the Unwinding

the Unwinding
and other dreamings

JACKIE MORRIS

In wren song, anticipation of nightingales,
hare's breath, pigment and word, this book
is dedicated to Robin Stenham.

Introduction

This book is not meant to be read from cover to cover. It is a book for dreamers. Slight of word, rich of image, its purpose is to ease the soul.

The images for *The Unwinding* were worked in watercolour over years, through time, in and out of books. They carried stories that were spoken only in pigment and never in letters. All were made as a way to unwind the tension brought on by the stresses of the everyday: work, home, life. Each image carries as many stories as there are people who look at them. The words in *The Unwinding* only pin one version to the pages.

The Unwinding is an invitation to shape-shift. It leaves space for the reader's imagination. The images and words are catalysts for the minds of dreamers and are not prescriptive. And yet were the book to be prescribed as a medicine, the prescription would read:

THE UNWINDING

***DIRECTIONS:* Take one story last thing at night before bed, then tuck the book beneath your pillow.**

For use in daytime, carry in a pocket or a bag. *Extra stories may be taken during times of stress.* **THERE IS NO DANGER OF OVERDOSE.**

SIDE EFFECTS: Can cause time to escape, bring relaxation to some, encourage dreams in others. Sharing the stories with others does not reduce potency, but can enrich the effects, especially when spoken aloud. Can be safely consumed by all ages and is also suitable for cats, dogs and other creatures.

J. MORRIS
APOTHECARY
nr. PEMBROKESHIRE
WEST WALES

But perhaps all this is just the hope and the wish of the author.

JM.

ONE

beginning

The Keeper of Lost Dreams

Does she have a name, this woman?
If she does, it is known only to a
handful of people. The bear knows.
He is the only creature of the earth
she would call her friend.
Between them there is trust, love.
Her world is between the dusk light
and the dawn light, the time of
the moths, of the owls and the bats.

The bear knows the scent of dreams
as they flow like small streams through the air,
and these streams are what they hunt,
what they follow to their source,
what they gather and bind.

Not a sweet scent.

Nightmares do not interest her.
She seeks only beauty,
though sadness charms her,
for
often the deepest beauty
can be found residing in sadness.

Wild dreaming is
what they desire most.
Dreams that hold the scent
of deep green moss, lichen,
the place where the roots of
a tree enter the earth, old stone,
the dust of a moth's wings.

All of these things and more
tell them of where they should go,
dreams they should follow.
Does she close her eyes and
breathe in the stream of a dream?
Is this how she catches them?
Only the great bear knows.

But if you wake to the light
to find beside your bed a book –
small, bound in beautiful covers –

then you will know that in the night they
travelled past, that you were dreaming,
even if the waking has swept
the memory of your dream far from you.

You will know they followed the scent,
stopped for a moment to gather your
thread to weave, wind and scribe,
colour your dream into their
Library of Lost Dreams and
Half-Imagined Things.

And you will know that before
they travelled on, she left you this gift.
A book of dreams.

TWO

solace

A Song of a Golden Hare

She cannot remember the first time she looked around to find a small hare following her. Intricately carved from gold, on a platform, thin, with delicate wheels, he was just there. Every time she peered around, a small flash of gold. In shape and form he was exquisite. Like a toy made for a faery's child. He followed her home and, as she slid the door open, slipped quietly past her and into her life for ever.

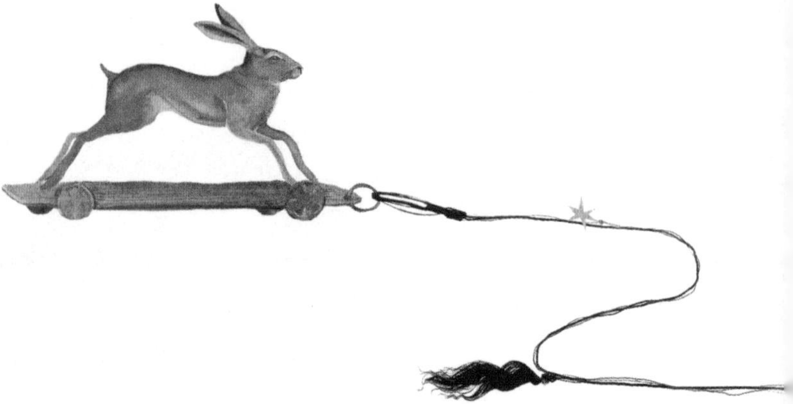

After a while, maybe hours, perhaps a few days, she found herself talking to the hare. At first just comments on how bright the day was, the beauty of cherry blossom, the touch of the wind. It came as no surprise when a soft voice spoke back to her. She did not feel that she owned him. If anything, it felt as if it were the other way around.

After a while she tied a loop of fine thread onto the hare's platform, so that it seemed, as she walked, not that the hare followed her, but that she pulled along this curious child's toy. If the people who saw her pass by failed to see how slack the thread was at all times, they never really remarked on this fact.

One day she asked the hare why he had come to her, of all people.

'Some questions,' he replied, 'are better left unanswered. There will come a time when you will have need of me. Then you will know.'

And yet she felt that she had always had need of him, that her life before this curious shadow of hers was insignificant. And often, in quiet moments, she wondered of the hare's life before they met, about who had made him, and how. But these were questions she found she could never ask, for when they reached her lips they vanished from her mind as rainbows dissolve in the light of the sun.

THREE

myth

The Midnight Fish

All she ever wanted was to escape
from the ground. Earth-bound,
landlocked, gravity her enemy.
All she ever dreamed was to lift light
into flight, to soar upwards, take to
the skies with winged things.

And birds. She loved birds – loved
how even a fallen feather, held
between fingers, would pulse and
turn in the hand and reach skywards
as if, like her, every feather longed to
be back in the air.

And, if she dreamed of him first, before ever they met, it did not surprise her, for she knew the power dreams hold.

And, if she dreamed him
into being, it would not
surprise her, for that very
same reason.

FOUR

shape

Dreams of the White Bear

I

When they spoke, the bear and the
woman, it was often in questions.

'What are the shapes of your dreams?'
she asked him.
'What do you mean?' he replied.
'Many things in one question . . .
what is the language of your dreams?
and, when you dream, do you dream
in words, images?
and, when you dream, are your dreams
colour, black and white, or colours
known only to dreamers?
are they visions, or something else?'
He asked, 'Something else?'
'Are they chemical, scent, touch?
What shape do your dreams take?
Do they have narrative, or are
they abstract?'
He closed his eyes, became lost in
thought. For a while there was silence
but for the sound of birds, the soft
breath of hares, a stir of winter leaves.

Later, as the moon rose and tangled in
the winter-bone branches of thorn trees,
she asked,
'Can you guide your dreaming?
can you move your dreams along
pathways of desire?
do your dreams shift in the spaces
between dreaming and waking? and,
when you wake, do you remember the
pathways your dreaming mind has
walked?
or do your dreams dissolve in the
light of each new day?'

She could not tell now if he was asleep
or awake, if her words were a lullaby.
And still she had more questions.

'Do you dream when you are awake?
do you imagine in words, in images?
do you wander the pathways of what
might have been, what might yet be
and all that you might become?
what is the shape of your imagination?
are dreams important to you, part of
the pattern of your soul?'

'Why do you wish to know?' he replied.

For a long time she searched her heart for an answer.

'To better understand the geography of my heart; how it fits with the pattern of yours,' she said.

FIVE

dance

The Winter Queen & Her Fox Lover

In summer heat he longed for her.
When leaves turned, green to gold,
he watched for her.
As winter came, on feathered backs
of redwing, fieldfare, and threaded
through the call of curlew,
he waited for her.

And when she came, earth under paw was iron hard.
And when she came, water thickened, turned to stone.
Flakes fell from a sky dark as a jackdaw's head.
She stole the colour from the land.
Frost feathered stone. Streams fell silent.

They danced. For three long winter nights.
They slept through the short times of light,
curled in each other's company.
She gave him gifts: a lapwing wrapped in feathers,
beaded with frost, a bowl of bright rosehips.

He gave her gifts: a crown of ice, woven with berries, feathers, and the light of love in his wild fox eyes.

When snowdrops speared the earth, he knew she would be gone. The skin on the water of the pond wrinkled, warmed. Ravens turned and tumbled in courtship in the smalt-blue sky. Celandine shone at the feet of hedge-banks. Wheatears rode the ocean of air and touched the land.

He woke in the dimity light of dusk to owl song and found her gone. Far across the valley the keen, yearning song of a solitary vixen called to his blood. The world turned.

SIX

moon

DREAMS OF THE WHITE BEAR

II

She asked him, What
is the scent of snow?
He replied,
Soft, cold, blue.
And she asked if blue
could be a scent.
He answered,
Moss, tundra,
clean earth and lichen.
The scent of snow is calm,
An absence of scent that
illuminates, so that any
warm life smells so rich.

Every flake carries its own unique shape,
and a scent to its path as it falls.

Snow mutes scent, he said. Cold steals
the scent from land, but also enlivens.
And, where ice meets sea, the salt scent
sharpens, water thickens.
Out on the ice, mineral pure, the scent of
snow is a sharp pain, a tightening of breath.

SEVEN

calm

The Midnight Fish

II

They swim in the air, these fish,
with their fins like sails, spending
their lives in search of moonbows –
those silvered arches that grow in
the sky when rain falls and the full
moon shines.
And these they will feast on,
until their scales glow bright
with the light.

And most times she follows them,
because once she saw one, curving
the air with its silvered colours
when she walked in the rain, in the
night, in search of a dream she had
thought lost, a story she needed,
to be complete.

Ever after she longed to find another.

And sometimes they find lost
and forgotten dreams, these
fish, silver-blue, indigo,
and these too they feast on,
from dusk light to dawn light.

Almost invisible in sun-bright
days, and yet you might catch
a glimmer, a shimmer of scale
or the flash of a tail.

EIGHT

peace

THE DREAMS OF BEARS

III

And so it seemed to her that he had always been a part of the landscape of her life, this great white bear.
She brought him rosehips to sweeten his days, tried to explain how, once they had been flowers, but now were seeds. He had never seen a rose.
He told her stories, coloured with every shade of white, and spoke of a sky that danced with lights.
She felt that he understood how the world began, how it might end.
And, even before they met, he walked in her dreams.

When he walked through her dreams moths rose from the earth where his paws touched the ground, as if born from his footfall. They followed him, a cloud of moths of all colours. And the music of moth wings followed him. And the dancing lights of the northern sky hung in his breath. In his eyes, a world of wild. On his coat, the colours of snow.
In his voice, the wisdom of untamed things.

And it seemed to him that she had always been a part of the landscape of his dreams, though for many years he could not understand her shape, until the day they met. So he told her the stories of colours and spoke with the gentle wings of moths, and walked through the world with her by his side. He loved this red colour of rosehips, like blood, but sweeter. She loved the light of wild in his eyes, the scent of frost in his fur and the movement of wings.

NINE

shelter

The Company of Wolves

Curled close in the curves of creatures,
she rests now. Warm.
Safe.

She has not forgotten the time she was lost –
how even while lost she refused to feel the fear,
but instead saw only the green beauty of the
wildwood, breathing deep the scent of trees,
earth, lichen, moss.

She followed tangled paths between tall trees,
sometimes a clearing, and here the sky a pool
of stars above,
sometimes trees so dense she had to make a
way through tangled briars.

And at twilight, when bats and owls flew beneath
the canopy of leaves, moths rose to greet the moon,
how the scents changed with the light of day.

Each path she followed led to beauty.
Stream, pool, waterfall,
rocks so thick with moss, bushes heavy with berries,
elder, blackthorn, sour crab-apples.

Even when she found the girl she refused to feel
the fear, though it tried to rise in her hackles,
and she met this life, so different from her own,
only with curiosity.

And when she followed Red and found the pack she knew only the joy of homecoming.

Curled close in the curves of creatures she rests now, warm, safe, in the company of wolves.

TEN

mirage

A Foxes' Wedding

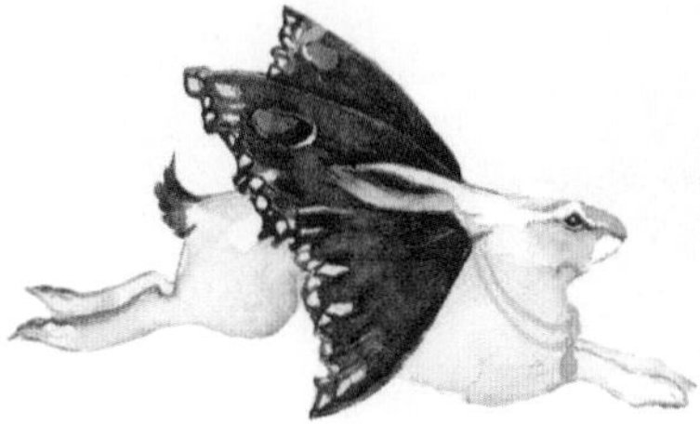

On the way to the foxes' wedding, snow.
Unseasonal, falling in sunshine.
The moon, pale as snow also.
Wings cold, despite the thin sunshine.
They move within the shapes of music,
the grace of dancers in their steps.
And, sometimes, such stories, dreams,
can only be told in questions,
can only be found in answers.

Where did they meet, fox bride, fox groom?
How long have they walked the land to the
rhythm of the music? When the snow ceases
to fall will the wedding begin?
If not then, when?
How can a hare grow wings?

What songs do they sing as the full moon
shines, almost transparent, in sunlight
and snow?

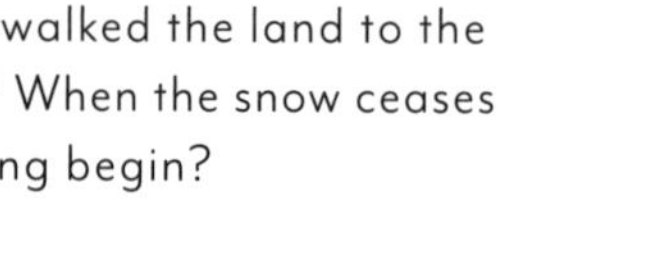

The answers live in the lands of dreamers, between a breath and a breath, in open hearts and open hands.

ELEVEN

harbour

A Strange Boat

If you stood on the shore and watched from
afar would you know how, beneath her hull,
two great feet propel her through the sea?
Wild, winged, she rests on the water.
Perched in cages, lit by lanterns, winged
dogs watch.
Soon they will hunt.

One blackbird sings.
Without her the sun will fail to rise and the
moon will never set.
There are times when she changes her song.

The women love to see the light of
the full moon in the daylight sky,
how it seems so slight,
almost transparent,
a tissue-paper disc in the light of the sun.
And they love to dance.

White bears guard their journey.
Dark-eyed owls watch the waves.
They are dreamers, these women,
these bears,
they are seers and speakers of truth,
dancers of time,
travelling the world, gathering stories.
For now, for a while, they rest on the water.

Stand on the shore and watch.
As the moon sinks towards the edge of
the sea you might see her open her wings
wide in the twilight and rise to the sky,
away from the skin of the sea,
into the ocean of stars.

TWELVE

truth

The Dreams of Bears

IV

She whispered into the ear of the dreaming bear.

If I said that my love for you was
like the spaces between the notes of a wren's song,
would you understand?
Would you perceive my love to be, therefore,
hardly present, almost nothing?

Or would you feel how my love is wrapped
around by the richest, the wildest song?
And, if I said my love for you is like
the time when the nightingale is absent
from our twilight world,
would you hear it as silence? Nothing?
No love?
Or as anticipation
of that rich current of music,
which fills heart,
soul,
body,
mind?

And, if I said my love for
you is like the hare's breath,
would you feel it to be transient?
So slight a thing?

Or would you see it as life-giving?

Wild?

A thing that fills the blood, and
sets the hare running?

THIRTEEN

hope

Out From the Woods

If they spoke of the Edge the People of the Forest spoke with fear, of the 'open world', of children at the Edge stepping out from the forest to be lost for ever, without the signs and the markers of trees to guide their way.

Inside the forest was safe, was home.

At the Edge and Beyond all was wild, and who knew what manner of monsters lived there?

So few of the People of the Forest had travelled in both worlds that many who lived their lives in trees believed the whole world was forest. To them the sky was a pattern of green and gold leaves, with sometimes, in clearings, a sickening height stretching deep and upwards into the skies. So many believed the Open World to be a myth, that there was no Edge.

But the Storykeeper knew. She had walked the lands of the Open, felt the land sickness that comes to those whose world is filtered through the green light of trees when exposed to a place with no shade, breathed that different air that did not carry the scent of leaves, had even looked upon places where few things grow, no rain falls and the earth shifts in the wind's hands without roots to hold it steady. She had felt the touch of the sun on her skin, unfiltered by the kindness of trees. And she knew that even there, far from forest, even there, small lives thrived.

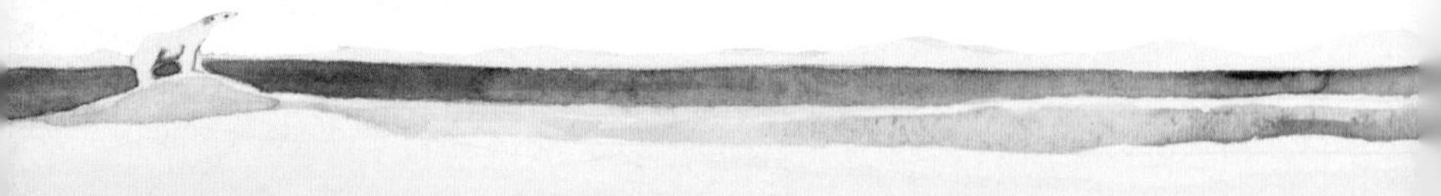

And now she knew it was time to leave for a while, not alone, but as a people. She who could speak in leaves and knew the language of birds, the history of the world, knew that it was time for a change.
And so they rode, out from the Woods and into the Open, with courage and with hope in their hearts, in search of an answer that might save their forest home.

FOURTEEN

rest

BEAR AND THE NIGHTINGALE

Wind in the trees,
rattle branch.
Can they hear the stars,
here where they lie
in the hollow?

Head in hands,
head on paw,
each rests in silent
trust of other,
while daylight moths
whisper night songs
and nightingale,
the bird of summer
threads his song of love
through winter's dark.

Hare loves the moon,
misses her bright gaze,
knows that she
will come again
with a wild certainty.

Blessing

Did she know, this woman who found rest in the peace of wild things, how the swan, who offered her body as soft pillow, had once been a maiden, caught in a rainstorm, crouched by the water in shelter of bushes, mistaken by her lover out hunting in twilight, who, seeing only her white petticoat thought her a swan and shot? Did she understand how, rather than falling, her wild soul had risen into evening light and flight in the form of a wild swan?

Did she know how the owl who guarded their dreams once was a woman made from flowers on a hillside – broom, meadowsweet and oak – to be a wife to one, but longed for another and was punished by those who failed to understand that a woman might prefer the freedom of flight, the night, the hunt, to the life of a wife?

Did she know her companion, the russet fox, her wild shadow, was Kitsune, the shapeshifter? And what of the grey wolf, who had carried a tsar across the sky to find a firebird, and the white horse who offered her strength and her courage? All of the stories she would learn as they travelled together, shared warmth as the snow fell, as the moon changed, as the stars pinned darkness to the sky.

Rest now,
in the peace of
the wild things.
May the swan be your pillow,
may the gold owl bring you visions.
May the red fox gift you cunning,
and the wolf bring you courage.

And may the white
horse lend her strength
to all your days.

ACKNOWLEDGEMENTS

With huge thanks to my agent, Jessica Woollard, for all the support and encouragement and for believing in me.

Also to Unbound, who see books as individual creatures, and especially to Lizzie Kaye, for understanding the curious pathways my mind wanders and for helping with the evolution of *The Unwinding*.

Thanks also to Alison O'Toole, designer, who listens, and then takes any ideas I may have had and then makes them as beautiful as they can be, with skill, and vision.

Thank you to everyone who pledged for this book, before they had even seen what it would be.

And also to the pack and the pride of those who share the days with me, Nicola Davies, who has taught me so much, and listens and knows when to offer advice and when to offer encouragement.

And to Robin... who always falls asleep when I read to him.

Unbound is the world's first crowdfunding publisher, established in 2011.

We believe that wonderful things can happen when you clear a path for people who share a passion. That's why we've built a platform that brings together readers and authors to crowdfund books they believe in – and give fresh ideas that don't fit the traditional mould the chance they deserve.

This book is in your hands because readers made it possible. Everyone who pledged their support is listed on the following pages.

Join them by visiting www.unbound.com and supporting a book today.

Independent Bookshops & Businesses

Books and Ink Bookshop, Winchcombe
Booth's Bookshop, Hay-on-Wye
Crediton Community Bookshop, Crediton
Elementum Gallery, Sherborne
Jaffé & Neale Bookshop, Chipping Norton
Kenilworth Books, Kenilworth
Norfolk Children's Book Centre, Norwich
Number Seven Dulverton, Somerset
Obsidian Art, Buckinghamshire
Point Reyes Books, California
Rocketship Bookshop, Salisbury
Rossiter Books, Leominster
Rossiter Books, Monmouth
Rossiter Books, Ross-on-Wye
Sam Read Bookseller, Grasmere
Solva Woollen Mill, Haverfordwest
The Edge of the World Bookshop, Penzance
The Literacy Company, Chester
The Old Chapel Gallery, Pembridge
The Old Electric Shop, Hay-on-Wye
The Poetry Bookshop, Hay-on-Wye
The Yellow-Lighted Bookshop, Nailsworth
The Yellow-Lighted Bookshop, Tetbury

A.

Lucia A.
Nerea A.
Ro Abberley
Emma Abbott
Tamsin Abbott
Sarah Ablitt
Yvonne Aburrow
Susan Adami
Lizzie Adams
Tricia Adams
Karen Aicher
Hilary Alcock
Holly & Grant Alden
Andrea Robin Aldridge
Sheila Algeo
Ahlyah Ali
Katherine Alker
Julie Allan
Christine Allen
Mia Allen
Seren Allen
Steph Allman
Marie-Louise Ambrosius
Alison Anderson
Jane Anderson
Judith Anderson
Sophie Anderson
Vicki Angel
Annora & Harris
Grant Cameron Anthony
Sarah Arkle
Sandra Armor
Brinder Armstrong
Jay Armstrong
Jane Arnold-Forster
Christine Arris
Keith Arsenault
Antonia Art
Wendy Ashley
Gordon Askew
John Atkinson
Katherine Attwell-Griffiths
Patricia Aubertin
Jennie Augustyniak
Janet Ayliffe
Grace B

B.

B
Nicole B.
Elfego Baca
Isabel Bachmann
Steven Badcott
Karen Badenoch
Mr. Badger
Shirlene Badger
Yaba Badoe
Duncan Baines
Anji Baker
Ellie Baker
Katy Balagopal
Linda Ball
Phil Ball
Deborah J Ballantyne
Jason Ballinger
Davina Balvack
Barbara Band
Amber Zephyr A Bankes xxx
Crystal Violet E Bankes xxx
Catherine Banks
Matthew Bannister
Leah Barabasz
Daryl Barber
Lisa Barber
Clare Barker

Helen Barker
Vivienne Barlow
Kate Barnard
Sally Barnett - InkyMotes
Lewis Barr
Sara Barratt
Archie Bartlett
Rosalind Bartlett
Laura Barwick
Sally Basile
Margaret Bateson-Hill
Diana Baur
Jan Baxter
Delia Baylie
Emma Bayliss
Nancy Baynes
Ruth Beach
S Beale
Anna Bear
Jane Beaton
Eli Beaumont
Bronwyn Becker
Petey Becker
Yvette Beckley
Catherine Bedford
Rachel Beer
Bernie Bell
Michael Bell
Victoria Bell
Sara Bellomi
Carolyn Belson
Kathryn Bennett
Susan Bennett
Django Bennett-Clarke
Lillie Bennetto
Elizabeth Bentley
Vicky Bernstein
Anna Berry
Heidi Berthiaume
Susie Bertie
Lisa Best
Bianca
Nikki Biddiss
Zöe Billings
Billy Boy
Heather Binsch
Louise Bishop
Linda Blackburn
Freddie Blackman
Cate Blackmoor
Cathy Blake
Valerie Blencowe
Sarah Blenkinsop
Laurel Bloch
Katharina Boehm
Amy Bogard
Cathy Bolton
Gilly Bolton
Velma Bolyard
Julia Bond
Justin Bonnet
Charles Booth
Mimi BoothbyTopo
Martin & Rachel Borgars
Nic Bottomley
Stephen Bowden
Mark Bowsher
Meri Brady
Milee Brambleby
Alan Brannon
Caroline Bray
Ciara Brehony
Lisa Brice
Aske Brock
Ellie Brooks
Moragh Brooksbank
Jenny Brophy
Pauline Brotherton
Myra Brown
Nadine Brown

Fiona Bruce
Jane Brumwell
Vyvyan Brunst
Bonnie Buckingham
Erica Bullivant
Susanna Bullman
Rachel Burch
Stephanie Burgis Samphire
Bonnie Ann Burnett
Nicki Burns
Bea Burslem
Tanya Butchers
Richard & Constance Butterworth
Janina Byrne
Susan Byrne

C.

Cecilia Cackley
Christina Cairns
Silvia Caldararu
Corin Caliendo
Paula Callus
Alanda Calmus
Elaine Cameron
Valerie Campbell
Melanie Cannon
Jennie Cappleman
Patricia Carberry
Elizabeth Card
Helene Cardona
Tricia Carey
Emily Olivia Cargill
Sam Carhart-Harris
Clare Carlin
Sandra Carpenter
Amber Carrasco
Derrin Cason
Cathy Cassidy
Jane Castner
Morwenna Catt
Carolyn Causton
Karin Celestine
Susan Chadwick
Dee Dee Chainey
Sarah Chalmers Page
Emily Chaplin
Claudia Chapman
John Luke Chapman
Elizabeth Charlesworth
April Chase
Ilona Chavasse
Khadim Chishti
Amelia Rose Chowdhury
Rebecca Christie
Suzy Clack
Annie Clare
Fiona Clark
Jeanne Clark
Joanna Clark
Alison Clarke
Julie Clarke
Lesley D. Clarke
Richard Clarkson
Lynn Clausen
Maddie Clayton
Sara Clemence
Cadi Cliff
Gill Clifford
Freyalyn Close-Hainsworth
Emily Clubb
Lizzie Clulee
Julie Coady
Lucy Coats
Philippa Cochrane
Caroline Cockrell
Alice Codner
Joseph Coelho

Annie Cogdell
GMark Cole
Helen Cole
Kate Collier
Alison Collins
Jennifer A. Comeau
Clodagh O Connor
Alison Cooke
Tessie Cooling
Edwards
Krista Coombs
Cathy Cooper
Denise Cooper
Fiona Cooper
Gaynor Cooper
Paula Cooper
Sheryl Cooper
Stephen Cooper
Karen Corfield
Emma Corfield-
Walters
Finley Corfield-
Walters
Brian Corrigan
David Corrigan
Andy Corsham
Glenda Cotter
Teresa Cotterell
Bob Cotterill
Elizabeth Coulter
Paul Counter
Amaryllis Courtney
Laura Covello
Cressida Cowell
Sian Cowper
Geoff Cox
Robert Cox
Tom Cox
Anne Crabb
Tina & Mike Crawley
Kathy Creamer
Christina Critcher
Sarah Crofts
Steve Cropper
Anna Crowe
Kate Crudge
Pat Cruse
Terry Culkin
Helen Culyer
Emoke Czako

D.

Robina D'Arcy-Fox
Jackie Daly
John Daniels
Elizabeth Darracott
Isabelle
Dasmahapatra
Beloe
Julia Daultry
Laura Davenport
David and Danielle
Helen Davidson
Cathy Davies
Harriet Fear Davies
Karen Davies
Nia Davies
Nicola Davies
Gregory Davis
Charlotte Hedwig
Dawson
Florence Anita
Dawson
Georgina Alice
Dawson
Joanne Day
Simon Day
Magdalena de
Banffy-Hall
Anne de Broise
Sheila de Courcy
Iva de Lasse
Ruby Deakin

Geraldine Deas
Michaela Deas
Nicola Dennis
Robin Denton
Penny Derbyshire
Willow Ivy Dewgarde
Lisa Dickson
Nicola Didsbury
Tracy Dillon
Valentina Dinca
Cathy Dixon
Emmeline Dixon
Catherine Djimramadji
Joanna Dobson
Nicola Dodd
Julia Doggart
Becky Doherty
Mary Alice Dooley
Marina Dorward
Jo Doswell
Laura Doty
Linda Doughty
dovegreyreader
Jill Doyle
Delyn Drake
Nick Drake
Caroline Driver
Orla Drummond
Rebekah Drury
Gail Duboe
Tracy Duddridge
Natalie Duffy
Susan Dulaney
Delia Dumont
Anne Dunn
Bev Dunne
Anita Dutton
Judy Dyble
Judy Dyke

E.

Imogen Ebsworth
Hugh Eckert
Raven Edgewalker
Faith Edman
Anita Edmonds
Rags Edward
Florence Rose Edwards
Jean Edwards
Mandy Edwards
Rachel Edwards
Rob Edwards
Sondra Edwards
John Egan
Eamonn Egginton
Amy Elizabeth
Marti Eller
Janice Ellis-Brown
Eloise Elluminations
Jo Elphick
Julie Emmerson
Anna Emms
F.A.C. Engelman
Elisabeth England
Sally England's
Betty Etienne-Fischer
Andy Evans
Danielle Evans
Gillian Evans
Kathryn Evans
Liz Evans
Adrienne Evetts
Megan Evetts
Suzanne Evry
John & Sue Exton

F.

Trish Fairbeard

Carlo Fanciulli
Jennie Faries
Susan Farley
Lucy Mary Farrell
Marlene Farrelly
Claire Farrow
Louise Farrow
Anna Farthing
Darci Faulkner
Lorna Fergusson
Poppy Fergusson
Cariad Stella Fetcher
Rebecca Field
Shirley Field
Rebecca Fifield
Pete Fillery
Ed Finch
Nicola Finch
Jane Fincham
Cathy Fisher
Simon Fisher
Rebecca Fisk
Catherine FitzGerald
Karen Fitzgerald
Andrew Fitzmaurice
Sorella Fleer
Elizabeth Fleischer
Harper Lynn Fleming
Fiona Fletcher
Miriam, Tom & Rose Flewitt
Marcheterre Fluet
Lisa Folan
Catriona Foote
Andy Forbes
Susan Ford
Helen Forshaw
Anna Forss
Angela Foster
Jane Foster
Charlotte Fox
John Francis
Philippa R. Francis
Sandra Frantz
Chris Fraser
Cissy Fraser
Shona Fraser
Alice Frebch

G.

Lucie G.
Majda Gama
Gillian Gamble
Saffron Gardenchild
Karen Garner
Fiona Elizabeth George
James George
Bärbel Gerdes
Ann German
Jetske Germing
Lauren Gerns
Chris Gerrard
Lyn Gibson
Sharon Gibson
Matthew Gilbert
Julie Giles
Shonagh Giles
Giles & Donna
Carol Gilham
Ruth Gilhooley
Carol Gill-Britton
Shauna Gilligan
Michael Gipson
Vivien Gledhill
Fiona Gleed
Jo Glen
Catherine Glenday
Mark Godson
Tahirih Goffic

Kate Gold
Stephanie Goldberg
Sarah Goldson
Kirsty Gordon
M Gordon
Margaret Gorman
Stephanie Gornall
Nancy Grace
Emma Lou Graham
Judith Graham
Terry Grant & Sue Emmert
Deborah Gravel
Amy Gray
Meridith Gray
Chris Green
Hannah Marie Green
Annie Greenlees
Peta Greenough
Denise Greenwell
Debs Gregory
Helen Griffiths
A Grime
Karyn Grimm
Sharon Grimshaw
Claire Grinham
Anisha Grover
Katy Guest
Emily Guille-Marrett
Sheila Guitard
S. J. Gum
Michele Gummett
Philippa Gurney
Zeynep Gurtin

H.

Stephen Hackett
Terri Hackler
Keith Hackwood
Sterling Hada
Kathrine Haddrell
Caroline Hadley
Milly Hadley
Linda Haecker
Julie Halgarth
Amanda Hall
Kirsty Hall
Dorothy Hallam
Constance Hamilton
Jackie Hamilton
Paula Hammond
Kersten Hammond-Reich
Conrad Hanchett
Nichola Hanman
Lindy Ann Hanson
Joan Haran
Hilary Harley
Anna Harlow
Andrea Harman
Candy Harman
AnneMarie Harris
Caroline Harris
Claire Harris
Emily Ruth Harris
Lynne Harris
Mary Harris
Jessica Alana Harrison
Mathew Harrison
Sally Harrop
D. Hartman
Karon A Hartshorn
Louise Hartwell
Gael Harvey
Tim Harwood
Tracy Haskell
Catherine Hatfield
Wendy Havelock
Leti Hawthorn
Tracy Hayes
Tim Haynes

Kate Haywood
Becky Hazelden-Brice
Kitty Healey
Jane Healy
Lindsay Healy
Ba Heap
Rebecca Heaton
Becca Heavrin
Giulia & Mick Heffernan
Sherry Helwer
Steve Hemmings
Vicky Hempstead
Ceacy Henderson
Rachel Henderson
Wendy Henderson
Vanessa M Heng
Helen Hennerley
Rebecca Hennessey
Mallory Henson
Lucy Henzell-Thomas
Di Hervey
Audrey Hetherington
Cecilia Hewett
Sheila Hewitt
Jay Hewlett
Clare Hextall
Elise Hibberd
Mary Hicks
Joan E Hill
Julie Hill
Lyn Hill
Stuart Hill
Laura Hill Smith
Helen Hillman
Charlotte Hills
Michael Hines-Mackay
Lindy Hinsley-Wintle
Susan Hinton
Henrike Hirsch
Elise Histed
Jacqueline Hitt
Robin Hobb
Anne Hodgkins
Penny Hodgkinson
Ann Hodgson
Yvonne Hodgson
Dennis Hollinghurst
Dell Hollingsworth
Kirsty Holmes
Lisa Holmes
Nikki Holmes
Jacob Hope
Beth Hopkins
Marcie-Jane Hopkins
Lisa Hopper
Avril Horn
Ellie Horne
Nia Horrocks
Katy Hoskyn
Diane Houdek
Lesley Houghton
Sue House
Susan Housley
Frances Howard-Brown
Catherine Howard-Dobson
Kath Hudson
Sue Hudson Craufurd
Lisa Huftel
Hilary Hughes
Nancy Hughes
Susan Hughes
Grace Jane Hulland-Spedding
Clare Humphrey
Elizabeth Humphreys
Jo Humphris

Suzanne Humphris
Heather Hurt
Geraldine Hutchins
Alice Hutchinson
Mark Hutchinson
Liz Hyder
Mary Hyland

I.

Jo Ireson
Ruth Irwin
Lisa Isaacs
Lisa Isaksson
Ann Ishiguro

J.

Robin Jacobs
Catherine James
Tracy Janine
Helen Jeffries
Davina Jelley
Vicky Jenkins
Lynds Jennings
Jill Jensen
Jill
Anna Joachim
Joe and Hamish
Anna Johansen
Charlotte John
Eva John
John & Deborah
Chris & Jacquie Johnson
H C Johnson
Jane Johnson
Joshua Johnson
Kim Johnson
Laurie Johnson
Sarah Johnson
Zoe Johnson
Zoë Johnson
Cathy Johnston
Anne Johnston & Micky Gibbard
Caitlin Jones
Eddy Jones
Elizabeth Jones
Kathy Jones
Laura Jones
Lesley Jones
Nancy Jones
Sarah Jones
Susan Jones
Theolyn Jones
Truus Joosten
Rachel Jordan
Mary Jordan-Smith
Mary Jowitt
Mary Jozwiak
Karen Jurgens

K.

Savita Kalhan
Eileen Frances Sheridan Kaner
Jennifer Kates
Carla Kaye
John Kaye
Lizzie Kaye
Sonja Keck
Jo Keeley
Pamela Kelly
Catherine T. Kelly & Laurel Masse
Meryl Kelsey Masters
Kendal
June Kendall
Aidan Kendrick
Christina Kennedy
Helen Kent
Laura Kepplinger

Mary Kersey
Rebecca Kershaw
Ruth Keys
Dan Kieran
Therese Kieran
Caitlin Kight
Laura Kilty
Belinda King
Eleanor King
Will King
Angela Kinghorn
Catherine Kirkham
Jackie Kirkham
Karen Kisner
Tessa Knight
Marie Knox
Kat Knupp
Jo Koszel
Giles Kristian
Barbara Kus
Rosa Kusbiantoro

L.

Amy Lacey
Sumitra Lahiri
Evelyn Laing
Pat Laing
Ann Lally
Jen Lammey
Philip Lancaster
Angela Lane
Helena Langford
Judy Langford
Puller Lanigan
Jean Larson
Sophie Lascelles
Katy Lassetter
Phil Latham
Rhiannon Law
Susanne Lawrence
Rebecca Lawrence-Crawshaw
Kim Le Patourel
Gwendoline Leach
Alison Lee
Amy Lee
Caroline Lee
Evalyn Lee
Linda Lee
Sam Lee
Maria Leibovsky
Fiona Leiper
Jacqueline Lensink
Fiona Lensvelt
M. G. Leonard
Ruth Leonard
Sandi Leonard
Alison Levey
Nora Levine
Lillian Levy
Cherry Lewis
Gill Lewis
Maria Jessica Lewis
Nicola Lewis
Rupert Lewis
Karen Liebreich
Susan Lim
Patrick Limb
Tracey Lindsay
Rose Line
Willow Line
Karan Little
Mark Little
Patricia Little
Andrew Liu
The Livocks
Joanne Livsey
Meriel Lland
Cathy Llewellyn
Tilly Lloyd
Cara Lockhart Smith
Linda Logie
Nancy Long

Zekie Loona
Sandra Lopacki
Wendy Lord
Racheblue Love
Catriona M. Low
Alison Lowe
Henry Lowther
Angelika Luethi
Nanzi Lyn
Rosa Lynas
Zoe Lynch
Michael Lynes
Brennen Lyons
Heather Lyons
Katherine Lyons

M.

Kim M
Susanna MacDonald
Karen Mace
Robert Macfarlane
Tracy MacLaren
Rhona MacLennan
Tracey Macleod
Bridgid MacSeoin
Susanne Madden
Vicki Madden
Sarah Madigan
Éabha Magorrian
Joy Main
Ruby Main
Emma Major
Deirdre Malcolm
Iris Malsom
Karen Manley
Caroline Mann
Hilary Manning-Morton
Keith Mantell
Laurie Manton
Ann Marchant-Daisley
Tracy Markey
Naomi Markham
Rebecca Marriner
Penny Marsden
Zoe Marsh
Deborah Marson
Kerry Martin
Lesley Martin
Lyn Marven
Lu Mason
Roan Mansel Casterton Massey
Charlin Masterson
Janice Mastorio-Worth
Anne Mattinson
Indigo Maughn
Barbara Mayes
Tonya Mayes
Rebecca Mays-Vandewater
Dara McAnulty
Mark McBride
Marta Dittert McCabe
Rebekka McCarthy
Trevor McCarthy
Ruth McCartney (ILY)
Yvonne Carol McCombie
Peter McCormack
Megan McCormick
Patti A. McDaisy
Jeanette McDermott
Helen McElwee
Lesley Mcfarlane
Fiona McGregor
Alana McKay
Amy McKay
Susan McKenzie

Catherine McKinney
Amanda McLachlan
Joy McLean
Sue Yin McMahon
Perry McManis
Amanda McMillan
Virginia McNamara
Claire McNamee Law
Jennie McNeill
Ri Meehan
Lily Isabella Meerman-Cooper
Abigail Mehmel
Barbara Joan Meier
Alice Meijer
Christina Meiklejohn
Patty Merrick
Susan Metcalfe
Jenny Metson
Alex Meyer
Patricia Michel
Sophie Midgley
Jane Midlane
Caroline Miles
Donna Miller
Jane Perrin Miller
Debs Mills
Allison Mitchell
Clare Mitchell
John Mitchinson
James Moakes
Alison Jessie Mold
Samantha Montes
Heather Montgomery
Jeanie Montgomery
Bel Mooney
Joanne Moore
Susan Moore
Laura Moorhouse
Sheela Moorthy
Vicky Moran
Suzanne Morgan
Wendy Morgan
Tamsin Mori
Polly Morley
Dr Helen Morris
Taylor Morris
Deb Morse
Conifer Morze
Mary Moss
Martha Mountain
Carol Mowat
Christine Mowat
Bernard Moxham
Nick Moys
Kirsten Mueller
Andrea Mugford
Beverley Mulholland
Ellie Mulholland
Diana Mullen
Kim Mullen-Kuehl
Thomas Mumey
Fiona Murphie
Barbara Murray
Gus and Julie Murray
Maureen Musson
Kirsten Muzeen

N.

Stu Nathan
Carlo Navato
Kirstie Nayegon-Bishop
Patrick Neale
Jeanette Neary
Jackie Needham
Anna Neill
Hilary Neilson
Larinda Nelsen

Dawn Nelson
John Newbold
Jeannette Ng
Ducky Nguyen
Hello Nguyen
Meran ni Cuill
Helen Nicholas
Deborah Nicholson
Julie Nicholson
Sue Nicholson
Freya Nicolson
Lasse Nielsen
Sally Nixon
Judi Noakes
Gwendolyn Noble
Claire Nodder
Susana Noguero
Emily Nolan
Natasha Nolan
Lynn Norfolk
Sally Norris
Meredith Norwich

O.

Hana O'Connell
Penn O'Gara
Ruth O'Leary
Mark O'Neill
Julie O'Rafferty
Vivienne O'Regan
Rebecca Ohl
Cam Christopher Omara Okwe-Pearson
Cassy Oliphant
Nick Olive
Ingrid Oomen
Jennie Orchard
Jay Osborne
Vita Osborne
Christoph Otto
Jo Ouest
Sharon Ovenden
Deborah Owen
Gary Owen
Menna Owen-Strong

P.

Hel P
Michelle Padula
Stephanie Palcich
Jane Palfrey
Martin Pallot
Sebie Palmer
Paula Palyga
Yi Pang
Jane Panton
Alberthe Papma
Vanessa Parkinson
Marcia Parks
Jeni Parsons
Kate Parsons
Erin Partridge
Caroline Morgan Passerotti
Val Patchell
Morag Paterson
Adam Patterson
Helle Patterson
Emma Payne
Krista Payne and The Multiverse at OneBlueOakPlace
Paula Payton
Lilly Pearce
Oliver Pearce
Martin Pearson
Nicola Peek
Karen Pendred
Grace Pengellt
Inmaculada Pérez Vázquez

Ben Perkins
John Perkins
Nadia Permogorov
Skylar Perry
Lesley Peters
Michelle Peters
Mags Phelan Stones
Karen Phillips
Kate Phillips
Clare Pierce
Karen F. Pierce
Kate Pierce-Myers
Liz Pilfold
Adriana Pisano Beaumont
Karen Pittaway
Linda Place
Caroline Platt
Anne Plowright
Sue Plummer
Sue Polchow
Justin Pollard
Karine Polwart
Rosalind Ponomarenko Jones
Freya Pope
Jenny Pope
Lynn Porfirio
Diana Porter
Rachel Porter
Emily Porth
Anabel Portillo
Joanne Pottage
Dion Potter
Rebecca Pound
Tracy Powell
Jayne Power
Roddy Pratt
Rebecca Prentice
Janet Pretty
David Prew
Joanna Price
Joan Lynn Primm
Wilfred Proctor
Karen Puffett
Victoria Pugh
Adele Pugsley
Christina Pullman
Catherine Purcell
Shanee Puri

Q.

Kitti Quarfoot
Caroline Quarmby
Lisa Quattromini
Jeannette Quigley
Nicky Quint

R.

Kimberly Rae
Carolyn Raffensperger
Jane Rainbow
Shelley Rainey
Jack Ramachander
Sandra Ramirez
Peter Randall
Morgen Raney
Anastasia Ratcliffe
Ellie Rattenbury
Jane Rayson
Penny Read
Ann Kilgore Reay
Ailke Shira Rechenberg
Emma Redin
Celia Rees
Bruce Reeves
Mia Carmen Reeves
Lara Reid
Eileen Reilly

John Reinhart
Angie Rekers
Betty Rembert
Barbara Renel
S.A. Rennie
Amy Reynolds
Jennifer Reynolds
Patricia Reynolds
To Ria & Rumi my Moon and Son. Love from Dada
Luigi Ricci Moretti
Simon Richards
Ali Richardson
Jane Richardson
Liz Richardson
Deborah Richardson-Webb
Seth Ridley
Daniela Rigamonti
Hannah Rigden
Erin Righetti
Jessie Riley
Katya Riley
Anne Ritchie
Julie Roberts
Marie Roberts
Gareth Robinson
Michelle Robinson
Lucy Rodger
Jonny Rodgers
Rachael Rodway
Anna Roe
Jenny Rogers
Kate Rogers
Niki Rogers
Elizabeth Reeves Rognier
Alice Rohdich
Michael Rohmann
Barbara Roidl
Jessica Rolfe
Elizabeth Rollo
Ronan n Griffin
Phil Rooney
Robyn Roscoe
India Rose
Vikki Rose
Tamsin Rosewell
Chrissy Ross
Linda Ross
Susie Ross
P Rotterdam
Kate Rouse
Rowena Rouse
Anna Route
Robert Rowe
Rachel Victoria Rowntree Clark
Jane Rudder
Lydia Ruffin
Melissa Rung-Blue
Sara Rushton
Fiona Russell
Joni Russell
Jennifer Russo

S.

Jacquelyn Saber
Linda Saboe
Evan Michael Saenz
Susanna Sale
Laura Salisbury
Emma Salmon
Lora Sampson Smith
Sarah Samuel
Samuel & Jess
Ellen Sandberg
Caroline Sanderson
Robin Sarner
Ruth Saunders
Kate Sayer
Ros Schell

Hannah Schmitt
Katrin Lena Schneider
Roz Schneider
Shari Schnuelle
Debra Schwyhart
Anne-Marie Scott
Kendall Sarah Scott
Matthew Scott
Suzanne Scott
Sylvie Scott
Oscar Searle
Annie & Mary Sedman
Claire Seeber
Alf Seegert
Caroline Senior
Lorna Senior
Carla Serenko
Anita Sethi
Marie Sewell
Karen Sewell, millinery artist
Julie Shackson
Eve Shaffer
Helen Shair
Harriet Shannon
Jody Shapiro
Cheryll Sharp
Matthew Shaw
Patricia Sheath
Eleanor Sheehan
Tara K. Shepersky
Gill Sheppard
Dearbhla Sheridan
Jadu Sheridan
Josephine Sherwood
Graeme Shilland & Jenny McLaren
Erika Shilling
Shirley's Library at Halberton Primary School
Dan Shlepakov
Claire Shovelton
Daniel Sibo
Emily N. Sibo Price Nilson
Sue Side
The Sidlaw Hare
Robert Siegle
Carolyn Sigman
Gurdyal Simm
Chris Simmonds
Heather Simmonds
Jane Simmons
Barbara Simons
Fiona Sinclair
Nicky Singer
Nesa Sivagnanam
McLeod Skinner
Lindsay Skudder
Christine Slade
Karen Slade
Debbie Slater
Annette Slokker
Caroline Slough
SmallTeethingBeastie
Steve Smart
Catherine Smillie
Carolyn Smith
Charon Smith
Clare Smith
Connie Smith
Gail Smith
Helen Smith
Jacqueline Smith
Lorraine Smith
Rachael Smith
Ruth Smith
Victoria Smith
Michael Smith & Nicky Parker

Julie Smithies
Elena Sokolova
Murielle Solsikke Solheim
Jo Song
Sin Soracco
Alison Souter
Leslie Sowden
Kit Spahr
Daisy Ma Specker
Sue Spence
Morgan Staden
Wendy Staden
Janet Stafford
Erin Stahler
Katie Stainsby
Kathleen Stalker
Karen Stanford
Aleksa Stanišić
Debra Mihalic Staples
Ruthie Starling
Brenda Steel
Shirley Steer
Ann Stenbeck
Robin Stenham
Betty Stenham-Brown
Clare Stenham-Brown
Jessica Stenham-Brown
Patrick Stenham-Brown
Ted Stenham-Brown
Cerys Stenham-Worth
Charlie Stenham-Worth
Meg Stern
Cody Stetzel
Linda Stevens
Ruth Stevens
Heather Stewart
Stickman
Borisse Stock
Christine Stockman
Amanda Stone
Aurora Stone
Sarah Stone
Allison Strachan
Sigi Štrauhs
Brigit Strawbridge
Kari Strebig
Hilde Stroobants
Pippa Stroud
Yasmin Strube @ Old Chapel Gallery
Julie Stuart
Susan Stuart
Kerry Stubbs
Helen Sturgess
Jill Sullivan
Sarah Sullivan
Nike Sulway
Beth Surdut
Jen Sutherland
Lynden Swainston
Aoife Swan
Romey Sylvester

T.

Jane T
Sabra Tarshes
Elspeth Tavaci
Annie Taylor
Becky Taylor
Brian Taylor
Charlotte Taylor
Dr. Rachel C. Taylor
Nicola Taylor
Siobhan Taylor

Jillian Tees
Charlotte Tefft
Isla Telford
Pamela Thom-Rowe
Heather Thomas
Joanna Thomas
Penny Thomas
Raynah Thomas
Sue Thomas
David Thompson
Helen Thompson
Liz Thompson
Mary Ann Thompson
Pen Thompson
Jo Thompson Coon
Kirsteen Thomson
Amelia Thorne
Roger Thorp
Kelly Throw
Becky Tierce
Liang Tiffany
Kim Tillyer
Kathryn Tipping
Anne Titsch
Pippa Tolfts
Lorna Toolis
Maile Topliff
Janice Torck

Jake Towers
Angela Townsend
Pam Traun
Jan Trenoweth
Lindsay Trevarthen
Sarah Trew
Adam Trodd
Jayne Truran
Chloe Truslove
Fran Tucker
Ann Tudor
Gail Tudor
Pip Tudor
Benji Theo Turner
Claire Turner
Dood Turner
Gabrielle Turner
James Turney
Leif Turpin
Curzon Tussaud
Ritambhara Tyson
Vangelis Tzanato

U.

Colin Udall
N Underwood
Claudia Unger
Clive Upton
Jennifer Uzzell

V.

Jo Valentine
Vicky van der Luit
Melanie Van Houten
Patricia van Ooy
Mark Vent
Shalu Verma Kumar
Gary Vernon
Kelly Vidal
Philippa Vigano
Sally Vince
Gale Vogeley
Roger Voller
Valhalla Voom

W.

Jo W
Elizabeth Wadsworth
Isabelle & John Waine
Christopher Wakefield

Beth Walker
Janet Walker
Jenna Walker
John Walker
Stephen Walker
Jamie Wallace
Nina Wallace
Matthew Walsh
Molly Walsh
Ali Walters
Gloria Walters
Kerstie Walthall
Emilia Grace
Walton
Jim Walton
Karen Walton
Claire Ward
Jennifer Ward
John Ward
Judith Ward
Philippa Ward
Wendy Ward
Amelie, Jessica &
Chloe Ware
Lora Waring
Abby Warren
Siu Ying Wat
Olivia Watchman
Ellen Waters
Paul Waters
Marry Waterson
Sarah-Rhiannon
Wathan
Claudia Watkins
Rob, Helen, Ava &
Martha Watkins
Deborah Watson
Janet Watson
Indigo-Syreni Watt
Naomi Watt
Chris Watts
Paul & Ann Watts
Sarah Weaving
Niki Webb
Sally Weed
Naomi Welch
Wesla Weller
Gini Wells
Karen Wells-West
Alexandra Welsby
Lorien Wendt
Mark Wentworth
Elsie Westmore
Katie Weston
Marianne
Westwood
Orla Whalley
Katy Wheatley
Alison Whelan
Pam Whetnall
Jenna Whinney
Mary Beth Whitaker
Georgina White
Karen White
Kirsty White
Susan White
White Bear Woman
Sheila Whitehead
Vicki Whitehead
Miranda Whiting
Jan Whittaker
Tina Whittle
Anne Whittock
Paula Whyte
Elaine Wickson
Heather Wiggin
Alison Wight
Jennie Wightman
Thomas Wigley
Fran Wilde
Matilda Wilding
Coulson
Danielle Wileman
Louise Wilkin

John Wilkinson
Dawn Will
Tracy Willans
Alys Williams
Amy Williams
Carol Williams
Donna Williams
Eleri and Tesni Williams
Elizabeth Williams
Gwynedd Williams
Jacqueline Williams
Judith Williams
Karen Williams
Kieran Williams
Lu Williams
Mark Williams
Poppy Belle Williamson
Sandra Williamson
Angie Willis
Laura Willis
Fiona Wilson
Jack Wilson
Terri & Howard Windling-Gayton
Nastassja Wiseman
Linda Witchell
Sharon Witt
Sophia Witte
Chandra Wohleber
Hanneke Wood
Trisha Woodcock
Susan Woodford
Tracy Woods
Sam Worby
Christine Wordsworth
Jordan Worrall
Laura Wreschnig
Alex Wright
Diana Wright
Kevin & Chris Wright
Michelle Wright
Rhian Wyn Harrison
Rhiannon Wyn Thompson

X.

Maria Xilouri

Y.

Jennifer Yates
Kate Yates
Ming-hsing Yen
Noel Young
Rick Young
Terri Young
Viv Young

Z.

Peedie Zoomie
Christine Zuber
Sunni Zuniga

First published in 2020

UNBOUND
6th Floor Mutual House, 70 Conduit Street, London W1S 2GF

www.unbound.com

Design by Alison O'Toole

Pages 8, 11–19, 23–33, 35–39, 43–49, 53–61, 65–71, 75–81, 85-91, 95–101, 105–111, 115–123, 125–131, 135–141, 145–151, and 155–179 composed and remixed by Alison O'Toole.

A CIP record for this book is available from the British Library

ISBN 978-1-80018-040-6 (Trade gift edition)
ISBN 978-1-78352-935-3 (Trade and special editions)
ISBN 978-1-78352-961-2 (Silent edition)

Printed in China by C&C Offset Printing Co., Ltd.

7 9 8 6

MIX
Paper | Supporting responsible forestry
FSC® C008047
FSC www.fsc.org